Runaway Teens

Other titles in the *Hot Issues* series

Cult
Awareness
A Hot Issue
ISBN 0-7660-1196-8

Cyberdanger and
Internet Safety
A Hot Issue
ISBN 0-7660-1368-5

Date Rape
A Hot Issue
ISBN 0-7660-1198-4

Drug Abuse
and Teens
A Hot Issue
ISBN 0-7660-1372-3

Eating
Disorders
A Hot Issue
ISBN 0-7660-1336-7

Endangered
Animals
of North America
A Hot Issue
ISBN 0-7660-1373-1

Hate and Racist
Groups
A Hot Issue
ISBN 0-7660-1371-5

Multiethnic
Teens and
Cultural Identity
A Hot Issue
ISBN 0-7660-1201-8

Sexually Transmitted
Diseases
A Hot Issue
ISBN 0-7660-1192-5

Stalking
A Hot Issue
ISBN 0-7660-1364-2

Teens,
Depression,
and the Blues
A Hot Issue
ISBN 0-7660-1369-3

Teens and
Pregnancy
A Hot Issue
ISBN 0-7660-1365-0

Teen Privacy
Rights
A Hot Issue
ISBN 0-7660-1374-X

Teen Smoking and
Tobacco Use
A Hot Issue
ISBN 0-7660-1359-6

Vegetarianism
and Teens
A Hot Issue
ISBN 0-7660-1375-8

The Women's
Movement
and Young Women
Today
A Hot Issue
ISBN 0-7660-1200-X

Chapter 1

Runaway Teens

A Hot Issue

Renée C. Rebman

HOT ISSUES

Enslow Publishers, Inc.

40 Industrial Road	PO Box 38
Box 398	Aldershot
Berkeley Heights, NJ 07922	Hants GU12 6BP
USA	UK

http://www.enslow.com

Library of Congress Cataloging-in-Publication Data

Rebman, Renée C., 1961–
    Runaway teens : a hot issue / Renée C. Rebman.
        p. cm. — (Hot issues)
    Includes bibliographical references and index.
    ISBN 0-7660-1640-4
    1. Runaway teenagers—United States—Juvenile literature.
[1. Runaways.] I. Title. II. Series.
HV1461 .R425   2001
362.74—dc21

                                            00-010854

Printed in the United States of America

10 9 8 7 6 5 4 3 2 1

To Our Readers:
All Internet Addresses in this book were active and appropriate when we went to press. Any comments or suggestions can be sent by e-mail to Comments@enslow.com or to the address on the back cover.

Illustration Credits: AP/Wide World Photos, pp. 30, 32, 43; Corbis Images Royalty-Free, p. 11; Corel Corporation, pp. 9, 22; Skjold Photographs, pp. 18, 27, 37, 38, 45, 46, 49, 56; TSM/Brent Petersen, 1999, p. 29; TSM/Charles Gupton, 1998, p. 15; TSM/Marco Cristofori, 1997, p. 25; TSM/Robert Essel, 1999, p. 3.

Cover Illustration: TSM/Robert Essel, 1999

Contents

A National Epidemic

"**S**ean," a fifteen-year-old teenager from Wisconsin, guesses he has run away from home as many as seventeen times. Sometimes his parents report him missing. Sometimes they do not.

Sean, who prefers not to use his real name, spends his days hanging out on the street with other runaways. Sometimes he smokes marijuana. He attends night school and hopes someday to get a high school equivalency degree. However, Sean has no other real plans for his life. He believes his father and stepmother care about him, but says that "they know I can take care of myself." Sean decides day by day whether he wants to return home or not.

Sean thinks he may be manic-depressive, a serious mental illness he has read about in a textbook. He goes through periods of intense activity in an excited state. Then he experiences extreme depression. He says:

> I don't sleep much. I won't sleep for a couple of days straight and then I'll crash for a while. My dad doesn't like it because he thinks I'm lazy. I could change it all—go home again and start

going to day school again. [But] every time I do it, a voice inside me says, "This isn't fun. This isn't what I want to do."[1]

It is estimated that about one to two million teenagers in the United States run away from home each year. Their average age is fifteen. More than half are female. While a lot of information is available about runaways, it is hard to pinpoint statistics about this growing problem. Some runaways are never reported, and many teenagers run away over and over again.[2]

There is no typical runaway. Each story is unique. Runaways come from all walks of life: single- and two-parent households; wealthy, middle-class, low-income, and even homeless families. They may run away from foster care, shelters, group homes, and other treatment or juvenile correction facilities.

Although the runaway problem crosses many boundaries and includes many situations, there is one fact that is true for all. The longer a teen remains away from home, the less chance there is of a successful return—and the more dangers the runaway is exposed to.

Who Runs?

Runaways can be roughly classified into two groups, situational and chronic (or long-term). About 70 percent of situational runaways return home within one week, typically after two or three days. Another 14 percent return within one month. Only about 5 percent stay away for a year or more.

Most teens initially run less than ten miles from home. Typically, most runaways will first go to a friend's or relative's house and are not in any immediate danger.

*R*unaways come from all walks of life. Many are drawn to large cities such as Los Angeles, San Francisco, and New York City.

Some teens run away repeatedly. If the problems that cause these teens to run are not resolved and they wear out their welcome wherever they are staying, they may be forced to move on. Then they might become long-term runaways.[3]

Some people believe that runaways are just delinquents looking for adventure. But Bob Husband of the Harris County juvenile probation department in Houston, Texas, says that "kids are running 'from' something in almost every case."[4] The problems they are running from are often serious: depression, school failure, substance abuse, physical or sexual abuse, or thoughts of suicide.

The crumbling of family bonds is often the reason teens choose to run. Many of these teens are simply looking for a place where they can feel safe and find someone to bond with. Long-term runaways often gravitate toward larger cities, where it is easier to blend in and possibly find other runaways to associate with.

Runaways are a problem in communities both large and small. New York City, Los Angeles, San Francisco, and other cities of this size are centers of activity for runaways—and that activity is not always legal. Detective Gordon J. Wendling of the Major Crimes Bureau of the Mansfield, Ohio, police department has experience in the juvenile division. He says, "Repeat offenders can be setting themselves up for a life of crime. Once criminal patterns develop, I do see [runaways with criminal records] later being picked up for adult offenses."[5]

The Slow Search

Usually, the police department is the first place parents or guardians turn to for help with runaway teens. But there is little the law can do unless a crime has been committed, the runaway has been victimized, or there are other special circumstances (for example, if the teen is sick or disabled). Running away is generally considered a minor offense, and the cases are not always actively pursued.

Bill Donovan of the Wisconsin Clearinghouse for Missing and Exploited Children knows at least part of the problem is financial. He says, "There isn't a police department in the United States that can afford to dedicate someone to a [runaway] case unless there's something unusual."[6] Trina Pace, a divorced mother in Edwardsville, Illinois, discovered that when her daughter, Candice Sharp, ran away.

*P*arents or guardians of runaway teens usually turn to the police first. Runaway agencies and hotlines provide another source of help.

Candice was dropped off to work at a Pizza Hut one day. However, she had no intention of staying there that day. Instead, she went in one door and out the other. She crossed the street to a van where a man she knew—a convicted felon on probation—was waiting to help her run away.

When she realized her daughter was missing, Trina Pace turned to the police. At first, the police felt Candice would phone her mother and return home on her own. Pace called the police daily, asking whether they had found out anything new or interviewed anyone from the list of names she provided.

Finally, eleven days after her disappearance, Candice's name was reported to the National Crime

Information Center. Director Ben Ermin said that Candice was certified as missing, and her case was put on their website a few weeks later. More than seventeen thousand law-enforcement agencies are able to access this up-to-date information. Candice's photo was also distributed through the center's national poster program.

Pace was frustrated at the slow progress of the search to find her daughter. She contacted about fifteen runaway agencies around the country, but felt like she was working alone. "You are on your own because runaways are a low priority for the police, and my experience in contacting the children's agencies was a slow process. Basically they did very little. I was doing the investigating myself."[7]

Pace also contacted the courthouse about the convicted felon and got his records and photograph. She found out that he was on restricted probation. His parole officer did not even know he was missing until she called.

Finally, Pace contacted Safe Kids International in Spring Lake, New Jersey. Safe Kids was able to get the information about Candice out on the Internet and made a poster offering a reward.

Joe Florentine, one of the founders of Safe Kids, says they currently have over sixty thousand points of contact that receive their information. They are hoping to expand their services. The program is privately funded. Mr. Florentine's dream is that eventually Safe Kids "will be funded enough to have a team of investigators so that when a kid is abducted we can immediately go into action with the police."[8]

Pace was lucky. Two and a half months after her daughter ran away, an apartment owner in Arkansas saw a Safe Kids flyer, recognized Candice, and contacted the police, who picked her up. Candice had been drifting around with strangers and experimenting with drugs. After returning home safely, Candice was hospitalized briefly and went into counseling. Her mother's persistent efforts had paid off.

It is often up to parents to find their runaway children themselves. Runaways are often mistrustful of agencies and reluctant to contact them for help. Until there is more funding and more help available for both parents and children, the runaway epidemic will continue to grow.

Why Kids Run

Often, teens who run away are facing circumstances at home or in their personal life that they feel they cannot control. The teen experiences a sense of helplessness, anger, and an inability to cope. When the teen can no longer handle the pressure, he or she chooses to run.

Teens sometimes run rather than facing problems at home or at school. A teen with poor grades may feel "bad" or "dumb," or may feel a lot of parental pressure to improve. Drug problems can also cause conflicts at home, leading to a desire to leave. Runaways may have no solid friendships and feel rejected by their peers. Sometimes they run to be with a boyfriend or girlfriend their parents dislike. They may run to get attention. They sometimes run to express their independence, to test their parents' love, or even to punish their parents.

Discipline in the household can be a major source of problems for teens. One teen described his parents' attempts at discipline:

> I've been running away from home since I was twelve years old, and each time my parents say I

*T*eens facing personal problems at home or at school may feel helpless, angry, and unable to cope. A teen whose problems seem overwhelming may choose to run.

can come back under certain conditions—always intolerable to me. . . . Cut my hair, stop wearing clothes I like, keep my door open—hassle on top of hassle. There isn't any conversation, only orders. There is absolutely no way I'd go back there. I'm happier without them. I want a family, not a master–slave relationship like I had.[1]

Single Parents and Stepfamilies

The trend of single parents raising children has had an effect on runaway statistics. These parents face many difficulties, both financial and emotional. They are sometimes unable to cope with or relate to a troubled teen. Ernest Allen of the National Center for Missing and Exploited Children believes that, in these cases, the problems that caused the teen to run tend to remain unresolved.

"We live in a time in which the stress and pressures on a single parent are enormous," Allen says. "But one of the complexities of this whole issue is that, in a lot of cases, returning the child home may not be the right thing to do. And resources to address chronic runners are limited."[2]

Changing patterns in households also play a role in the increasing numbers of runaways. Many kids are growing up in families where their own two parents no longer live together. They have to deal with stepparents and stepsiblings. This can be upsetting to a teen already facing major life changes.

Divorce and remarriage affect the way parents and children relate to one another. While their parents build new lives, teens often feel abandoned. They yearn for an emotional connection they feel has been lost. Their environments often lack the stability they need to learn to function well and to succeed. Teens living in these nontraditional family structures are less likely to attend college. They have a greater chance of running away and are less likely to return home.[3]

Emotional reasons are not the only factors causing these teens to run. They often face terrible abuse from stepparents, stepbrothers, or stepsisters. A large number of these runaways are abused, many of them sexually.

Detective Wendling finds that runaways are not always willing to confide about being abused. "Sometimes they'll open up to you and sometimes they won't," he points out. "Allegations made by runaways can prove not to be true, but if you don't ask, you don't know. When abuse by a parent or stepparent is suspected or other suspicious circumstances are involved, it can lead to a criminal investigation. Allegations are taken seriously."[4]

Sixteen-year-old Jean ran from an abusive situation when she was thirteen. She crossed several states to escape. She drifted from her best friend's home to a boyfriend's and then to a cousin's. Jean does not want to return to the frightening home life she describes. "It was very abusive at my mom and dad's house—physically, emotionally abusive. My stepfather is crazy. He's like this total alcoholic and a big pothead. Whenever he was drunk, he'd chase after us with guns!"[5]

Natural Parents

Eva, a fourteen-year-old runaway, also escaped a dangerous home situation. Her mother, who was an alcoholic, physically abused her. When Eva decided to leave, she stayed with a friend in what turned out to be a crack house. Addicts would come to the

Project Safe Place

Project Safe Place was begun by the YMCA in 1983. It encourages teens not to run and gives runaways a way to get off the streets. Safe Place signs are posted at participating fire stations, stores, and other locations. When a teen comes to a Safe Place location, a staff member or volunteer is sent to the site to provide assistance. The parents are notified as soon as possible.

Cities around the country that have adopted this program find that teens in trouble are more likely to ask for help when a Safe Place is available to them. The program is designed to catch teens in the early stage of a crisis and help them find lasting solutions to their problems.

In 1986, President Reagan recognized Project Safe Place with a Presidential Citation. The program was cited as an excellent example of business and nonprofit agencies combining efforts to improve the community.[6]

apartment to buy, sell, and use drugs. While Eva was there, a visitor to the apartment raped her.

Eva ran to the police for help, even though she knew her parents had reported her as a runaway. Eva's warrant was tracked through the Department of Social Service and she was returned to her parents' home. But she did not stay there long. After a few days, Eva ran away again. She ended up in a shelter and hoped to be placed in a good foster home. Eva longed for the love and nurturing she did not receive from her own mother.[7]

Teenagers facing abuse at home often have conflicting emotions. They are angry and afraid, yet most report that they still love their abusers. Their need to feel loved and accepted outweighs the risk to their personal health. They remain at home, hoping the situation will change. Many cannot or will not defend themselves.

One sixteen-year-old runaway, Gretchen, suffered severe physical abuse from both her mother and father. Yet she said she would not hit back even while she was being attacked. Gretchen recalled one horrible incident involving her mother:

> She was choking me . . . but I did not hit her back. I called her a name and that was it. When I tried calling the cops, she hung up the phone and started punching me. After she was done hitting me, she yelled at me for an hour.

Gretchen ran away and ended up "in the system." Social services put her in a shelter. She was scared and worried about what would happen to her, but kept telling herself, "anything is better than being at home." Gretchen knew her personal survival was at stake.[8]

Although shelters may be safer than the homes runaways leave, many will not stay. They view being in the social services system as too frightening. They feel they have lost control over their own lives— control they so desperately need. Their mistrust and fear will not allow them to accept the help being offered.

Teens often run from shelters, foster homes, group homes, and juvenile correction facilities. Yet when a teen is receptive to help, these same facilities can provide a turning point in their lives.

A Shelter Helps

Michael had run away many times, eventually ending up in a foster home. Unfortunately, his foster mother assaulted him in front of others in the home. Michael felt he had been shamed and ran away. While living at home, he had been in constant conflict with his younger sister. He felt no matter what he did, his mother favored her. Whenever a problem arose, he felt that his mother took his sister's side. Michael's jealousy, anger, and resentment grew until he felt he had no choice but to leave. Instead of running again, he asked his social worker to get him out of his home.

He was sent to a shelter and began to connect with his peers and with the community workers there. Michael had finally found a place where he felt good. He no longer wanted to run. He admitted he loved being at the shelter and wanted to stay because "everybody treats me respectfully here." The system finally worked for him. Michael found a new beginning.[9]

Chapter 3

Throwaways

While most teen runaways choose to run, many are forced to leave homes where they are no longer welcome. They are known as throwaways.

Teens may end up in throwaway situations for many different reasons. Some teens are asked to leave because there is no money or not enough resources to care for them. (The rate of teen throwaways tends to increase during economic recession and periods of inflation.) Facing financial problems, their parents make it clear that it would be better if the teen were gone. They see the absent teen as one less mouth to feed. A counselor at Runaway House in Washington, D.C., has seen many such cases:

> Very often kids are kicked out of a home when they would really like to be there. Sometimes parents have so many problems they scapegoat the child. He may be some trouble, and parents going through hard times just don't think it's worth it to feed and clothe him anymore.[1]

Throwaways are different than runaways. They have no home to return to. In the case of one very

Throwaways

A recent study by the U.S Department of Justice yielded the following statistics about the problem of throwaways.[2]

✓ Among throwaways, 84 percent were sixteen to seventeen years old. By comparison, only about 67 percent of runaways were of that age.

✓ There were about as many girls as boys.

✓ Nearly half of the throwaways had been asked or forced to leave their homes.

✓ In another 25 percent of these cases, the teen had run away but the parents or guardians did not care whether or not the teen returned.

✓ For an additional 29 percent of throwaways, the parents or guardians of a runaway teen had made no effort to recover the teen.

✓ Almost 68 percent of throwaway teens did return home within two weeks. But under these conditions, it is likely the teens would run again or be forced out.

young throwaway, the reason he was asked to leave home was never made clear. Eleven-year-old Richard was thrown out of the house by his mother. His mother said she couldn't take it any longer, but she never explained what "it" was. Richard spends his days roaming the streets of Albuquerque, New Mexico. According to Richard:

> I just hang out. I stay in parks when I can't crash somewhere, sometimes Roosevelt Park, or the graveyard toward the airport. It scares me, though. I think someone might kill me while I sleep. I ain't too big a kid, you know. There's nothing to do. I keep thinking someone will adopt me.[3]

Some teens are asked to leave because of their own disruptive behavior. Their drug abuse, violence, or disciplinary problems cause severe conflicts within the home. In some cases, parents become disinterested in helping the child and no longer wish to put up with the strain on the family. Mike Edler, a police officer in Madison, Wisconsin, has seen instances where families can no longer handle teens in trouble. "There is a percentage of kids—I don't call them runaways, I call them throwaways," he says. "They've gone through social services. They've gone through two or three counselors. To keep peace in the family, the parents say, 'Get out of here.'"[4]

Changing Behavior

These teens are well aware of the problems they are causing in the home. Yet they are unable or unwilling to alter their unacceptable behavior. These throwaways know their parents will not allow them to return home unless changes are made. Even though the teen may want to return home, he or she is unwelcome. Gregg's story is typical of these cases.

Gregg left because he felt no one cared for him. He misses his home and yearns for a reconciliation with his father and stepmother. He maintains contact with his family and arranged a visit with his father. Their time together was pleasant, but his father does not want Gregg to return:

> Sunday was the first time I've seen him. . . . We went fishing and talked about all this stuff. It was pretty good. He won't let me back home, but that's . . . because he doesn't feel I'll get along there. He's afraid of something that I'll do. He's afraid I'll hurt my mom or sister or something. I'm not a violent person at all . . . but he's strongly against me coming back home. It's a little painful, but I just blame myself for that. I was off doing my own thing—drugs, basically.[5]

Conflict is evident in Gregg's words. He claims his father's fears are unfounded. But Gregg knows his drug abuse is blocking any chance he might have to return to his family. He chooses to continue his damaging behavior and refuses to change. In the meantime, he will remain a throwaway statistic.

When Parents Are the Problem

Another surprising twist in the case of throwaway teens are instances where the parents are the substance abusers. They feel that their lifestyle is hindered by having a child around. They resent their parental responsibilities or even refuse to acknowledge them. They expect the teen will simply go along with whatever they wish to do, even steal for the parents to support their habit. When the teens refuse to help their parents or accept their parents' behavior, they are told to leave.

*T*hrowaways often have no real home to return to. Their parents or guardians may have asked them to leave—or may not care if they ever return.

Voyage House, a center for runaways in Philadelphia, has dealt with these cases. Executive director Susan Pursch reports, "We're seeing a relatively new group of young people whose parents are the substance abusers, the ones taking the money. The kids say 'no' and parents toss them out."[6]

Throwaways are of particular concern to police, shelters, and social service agencies. Even if the parents could be persuaded to take the teen back, in many cases the teen would be facing a hostile environment. It would not be in their best interest to return home; they would have nothing to gain by going back. And sadly, most throwaways have nothing left to lose. Throwaways are truly a lost segment of the runaway population.

Chapter 4

Life on the Streets

Teens who become chronic runaways usually end up on the street. They are then faced with the harsh reality of day-to-day survival. Life on the street is brutal. The dangers faced by a runaway are numerous, and time is an essential factor in determining what will eventually become of them.

Charles Pickett is a case manager at the Arlington, Virginia, headquarters of the National Center for Missing and Exploited Children. "The more time passes, the hungrier they get," he points out, "and the more likely they are to get raped, commit a crime, break in somewhere, get hurt or get in some kind of trouble."[1]

Without a high school diploma, finding a good job is nearly impossible. Shelters and soup kitchens do offer free meals in various locations, but runaways often end up stealing food to survive. Some get their meals by "table scoring" at fast food restaurants. They grab unattended leftovers before they are thrown away. "Dine and Dash" is another

*R*unaway teens may be able to find food at homeless shelters and soup kitchens. Many runaways, however, end up stealing food to survive.

popular method of getting a meal. The runaway eats in a small diner or restaurant, then runs out the door without paying for the meal. Others engage in "Dumpster diving." They go through the large garbage Dumpsters behind restaurants to find food that is still edible. Many are regulars, routinely scavenging from the same Dumpster.[2]

Many runaways also have their first experience with sex and drugs once they become immersed in their new lifestyle. Substance abuse is rampant. The highest percentage of drug abuse among teenagers occurs among runaways trying to make it out on the street. Approximately 75 percent of street youths report using marijuana. Around 33 percent admit to using hallucinogens, and about 25 percent say they use crack cocaine. Intravenous (IV) drug use is reported by 17 percent.[3] (Intravenous drug use involves injecting a drug into a vein with a needle.)

Runaways, both male and female, often turn to prostitution to support themselves or their drug habits. Because of this, there is a high percentage of HIV infection among runaways. But AIDS is only one killer of street kids. Alcoholism, drug overdose, and homicide also claim many lives. Runaways must accept these things as part of their fate. Most do not believe they will live long. They see life on the streets as harsh and short.

One sixteen-year-old boy described the fear and despair he felt when he was hustling his body on Santa Monica Boulevard in Hollywood, California. "You don't know how scary that is," he said, avoiding eye contact. "You don't know if you're going to be shot, stabbed or taken to Mexico."[4]

Train Hopping

Runaways sometimes ride the rails with no particular destination in mind. Evan Karl Cutler tries to discourage this practice by telling about train hoppers in his autobiography, *Runaway Me: A Survivor's Story*:

> Train hopping is an adventurous but dangerous way to travel. A girl in this town recently lost her grip from a slow moving train and sacrificed both her legs in the process. If you succeed in hopping a train, you then have to figure out how to get off. The trains pick up speed, exposing you to viciously cold sixty mile per hour winds, and may not stop anywhere you'd want to be for days. Hoboes who travel the rails are known for being quite violent to train hoppers they don't accept. If they catch you, railway police will arrest you. I don't advise this method of travel.[5]

*L*ife on the streets is harsh and dangerous. Shelters are able to help only a small percentage of homeless people. Others have to fend for themselves to find food and a place to sleep.

Troubled teens often end up in big cities like New York, San Francisco, and Seattle. But the city with the largest runaway population of all is Hollywood, California. Experts estimate that there are ten thousand homeless kids on the street on any given night in Los Angeles County. As many as three thousand of them are in Hollywood alone. The Hollywood shelters can only accommodate a very small percentage of those in need. Runaways are lured to this city by dreams of stardom and the knowledge that thousands of others like themselves are already there. All too soon, however, runaways find their dreams shattered.

Alone in Hollywood

Christine was fifteen years old when she ran away from her Louisville, Kentucky, home and headed for the West Coast. She came from a middle-class family where violent fights erupted from time to time, often leading to 911 calls.

After making a New Year's resolution to escape, Christine snuck out of the house at 5:00 A.M. on January 2. She brought $144, two cans of soda, six cans of tuna fish, a jar of peanut butter, her diary, some clothes, a pocketknife, and a photo of her eight-year-old sister. Christine took a bus to Hollywood. She says, "I sort of figured that anybody could get by in Hollywood. Lots of freedom and good weather and stuff."[6]

After a short while on her own, she was low on cash and decided to try selling her body on Sunset Boulevard. Christine was chased away by the prostitutes who frequented the street. A week later, down to her last seven dollars, Christine tried prostituting again with no luck. She felt her appearance was working against her. "I was wearing jeans, which were dirty, and I was carrying my backpack, so I guess I didn't look right."[7]

Christine got her spare blue jeans out of her backpack and cut the legs off using her pocketknife. She began walking the boulevard in her new shorts, mimicking the actions of the prostitutes she saw. Soon, a man in a blue car pulled up to the curb. Christine got in and was driven to a nearby motel. She was too nervous to discuss payment. The man dropped a few bills onto the nightstand and began to undress. Christine remembers how horrible she felt:

The city with the largest runaway population in the United States is Hollywood, California. Many teens are lured there by the promise of good weather and dreams of stardom, but quickly find their dreams shattered.

I couldn't do it. I wanted to run. I just started crying. It was like the man was really, really embarrassed. He was older than my father even, and I couldn't stand it. He asked me to please, please stop crying, but I couldn't. So he just gave me ten dollars and walked out, saying he'd never touch a kid who was crying.[8]

Two weeks later, Christine turned sixteen years old. Within four days of her birthday, she turned her first trick. She became one more Hollywood prostitute working the streets. Yet she claims, "At least it's better than living at home."[9]

Prostitution

Pimps often prey on young runaways to prostitute for them. They hang around the bus terminals and train stations waiting for new runaways to arrive. The runaways are easy to spot, says an outreach worker named Seven. "You can tell them by their clean shoes and backpacks and that scared look on their faces."[10]

Pimps will quickly befriend these teens, particularly the girls. They take them to their homes or apartments, buy them food and clothing, and give them what they crave the most—attention. It does not take long for the runaway to grow to trust the pimp and depend on him for money and emotional guidance. At this point, typically, the pimp asks for sex, and the young girl complies. After a while, the pimp might force the girl to have sex with his friends or put her directly to work on the streets turning tricks. All the money earned goes to the pimp. Since the pimp controls the money, it becomes difficult for the prostitute to ever leave him.

Pimps also use the tactic of getting their

The Streetcats Foundation

While many runaway crisis centers are available for teens seeking help, the Streetcats Foundation brings the help to the teens. Originally organized in 1988, Streetcats works with at-risk kids and runaways on the streets of New York, Philadelphia, Los Angeles, and San Francisco.

Streetcats workers cruise the toughest streets of the cities in blue-and-yellow jeeps, interacting with teens in trouble. They offer help to get the teens off drugs, out of prostitution, reconciled with their parents, and leading productive lives.

Streetcats also produces the national radio public service announcements "Through the Eyes of a Child." Streetcats runs the National Children's Coalition, an educational organization for children and youth workers.[11]

prostitutes hooked on drugs, serving as their supplier. They become the prostitutes' only source of protection, bailing them out of jail if necessary. Pimps also intimidate prostitutes through violence. The frightened teens obey the rules, feeling they have no other option.

It is far more common for young male runaways to prostitute for themselves. The males face the same dangers of rape and assault as the female prostitutes. As they age, both sexes find it more difficult to continue prostituting themselves. Younger prostitutes are the ones in demand. Many eventually turn to other crimes to survive, such as panhandling, robbery, and drug dealing.

Other Crimes

Panhandling, or begging for money from strangers on the street, is relatively simple and generally safe. Although panhandling is against the law, the police do not often bother panhandlers. Runaways can sometimes make ten or twenty dollars for a few hours of begging.

Petty theft and shoplifting are also practiced. Runaways do not only steal items for themselves to use, but steal things they hope to return later for cash or sell on the street. Even when caught, they are sometimes turned loose when stores do not bother prosecuting them. But, eventually, some runaways turn to more serious burglaries and larceny and end up spending time behind bars.

Drug dealing is a common crime for a large portion of runaways who use drugs. They will often trade sex for drugs to sell on the streets. Sometimes they obtain their drugs by prescription from dishonest doctors. After filling the prescriptions at a pharmacy, they sell the drugs for a huge profit to be shared with their supplier. Sooner or later, selling drugs usually leads to arrest and a police record.

Street Families and Squats

Runaway teens often group together for support and protection. These groups are sometimes known as street families. These families try to protect and help their members. For a young runaway who may have experienced severe problems at home, the support of a street family is welcome. Unwritten rules and codes of conduct dictate what type of behavior is tolerated. Stealing from a member of the family is not allowed. Anyone disrupting the group is kicked out and shunned. But even the strongest of street families does not usually last long. The leader may be arrested, or fights between members can break up the unity of the group. Pregnancies or drug overdoses can cause insurmountable difficulties. Then the runaways are forced to find another group to join.

Sometimes teens find themselves living with others who have no concern for their welfare at all. They are simply sharing the same space in an abandoned building known as a squat. Several dozen teens may inhabit these places at once. There is no running water or heat or electricity. There is no furniture. The inhabitants sleep on bare, dirty mattresses or on the floor. Rats run through the corridors. Human waste, garbage, and used hypodermic needles collect on the floors. Maggots and flies infest the spoiled food that is left lying around. Yet these squats are often the only alternative to park benches and back alleys. Police make periodic raids on these squats to chase the inhabitants away. But it is only a matter of weeks before the teens return.

Living in a squat can be dangerous. Crack and heroin addicts pose a serious threat to other runaways. There is always the very real chance of being molested or hurt while sleeping or being robbed of one's belongings.

A sixteen-year-old runaway girl from Houston, Texas, who goes by the street name of Green, lives in a squat in Hollywood. She does not talk about why she left home but hints at having come from a middle-class family. She previously attended private

*R*unaway teens may find themselves sharing an abandoned building, or squat, with several other homeless people. Squats can be dangerous places to live and are often strewn with garbage and drug paraphernalia.

*T*he odds are against survival for teens on the street. Many die without their families ever knowing.

schools and took piano and trumpet lessons. She now takes hits of acid and panhandles from tourists on the street. Green is thin and dirty; her head is partly shaved with three rows of spiked hair.

The entrance to her squat is a boarded window eight feet up from a garbage-strewn alley. She must use a broken metal railing to gain access and pull the plywood back. By dropping down into what used to be a bathroom, the toilet and tub now filled with human waste, she makes her way to the room she shares with her boyfriend, Troll. Their only furniture is a single chair. The stench is overpowering, but Green claims she is used to the smell.

Speed freaks, known as "tweakers," and crack addicts are the most dangerous residents in the building. Green says, "Sometimes they'll crawl along the floor through the garbage looking for drugs."[12] One young tweaker, a girl with her head partly shaved, stumbles down the hall, jabbing a metal bar into the walls over and over again.

Despite what Green sees, she is tempted to try stronger drugs. "I [want to] try heroin tonight," she declares. "A friend says she'll shoot me up, but I'll need to get ten dollars." Her boyfriend, Troll, does not do drugs. He wants to know why Green wants to try heroin. Her reply is simple. "I just want to see what it's like."[13]

There is no real safety for street kids, only survival. And the odds against that are high. Many will die without their family even knowing. Most of these kids adopt street names and their true identity is lost. Several thousand unidentified teens die each year in the United States. They are buried in plots for the poor and forgotten. Their deaths are as lonely as the street lives they led.

Chapter 5

Getting Help

Police often have the first contact with runaways. They have special training to deal with them. "Parents sometimes request the child be brought home instead of entering into the system," according to Detective Wendling. "When that is done, after the runaway is interviewed, I sit down with the parents and the child to try to discover why the child ran in the first place. These meetings are emotional," he continues, "but they can help. Parents have, on occasion, contacted me later to thank me, saying my counseling made a difference."[1]

Special Resources

Sometimes more structured assistance is necessary. There are many organizations and programs dedicated to helping runaways. Although more resources are needed to combat the growing problem, help can be found for teens as well as for family members who want assistance. Some programs offer temporary places of residence as well as counseling services. Many programs serve as a mediation point between runaways and their families. Others offer hotlines to provide information or simply someone to talk to. A positive outcome to runaway situations is more likely when these types of resources are used.

One nationwide service, the National Runaway Switchboard (NRS), was established in Chicago in 1974. It receives more than one hundred twenty thousand calls a year on its toll-free hotline. Their phone number is circulated to schools, agencies, and shelters. It is often posted in public places as well, such as the bus and subway terminals that runaways frequent.

Trained volunteers handle the telephones, and

A Call for Help

These statistics are based on calls to the National Runaway Switchboard in 1998. They show the length of time runaways had been on the run when they placed the call. The data suggest that runaways who call for help are most likely to do so early on.[2]

0-3 days	39%
4-7 days	22%
1-4 weeks	15%
1-6 months	19%
more than 6 months	5%

all calls are strictly confidential. The fact that a caller can remain anonymous encourages some teens who might not reach out for help otherwise. Once the teen feels comfortable, the process can move forward. If requested, the NRS can arrange conference calls between parent and child. They can deliver messages if no direct contact is desired. The NRS can be the first point of contact and the first step in reuniting runaways with their families.[3]

Programs that offer shelter along with counseling services have a good rate of success in dealing with runaways. Along with getting runaways off the street, these programs generally strive to help them resolve immediate problems as well as develop plans for the future. The Family Connection Halfway House in Houston, Texas, was one of the first of such shelters in the country. Their positive statistics reflect the good work they do. They report that about 50 percent of runaways who receive counseling there return home. Around 30 percent set up their own households, and 10 percent join a group-living situation. About 10 percent end up back on the streets. Halfway houses such as Family Connection are very helpful to runaways. Unfortunately, there are not enough of them in operation.[4]

Some runaways, because of trouble with the law, end up in locked down juvenile detention centers. There they serve sentences for a specific period of time. As an alternative, teens committing less serious offenses are referred to voluntary shelter houses by the State Department of Social Services. These residences are not locked down. But runaways cannot simply drop into these types of facilities. They must get a referral from the State Department of Social Services or the Department of Youth Services

The Home Free Program

Greyhound Bus Lines offers a way home to any runaway teen in the United States. Teens between the ages of twelve and eighteen can receive a free bus ride to any of Greyhound's 2,400 locations through a simple phone call. By contacting the National Runaway Switchboard at 1-800-621-4000, the center will make arrangements with Greyhound for free travel.

Local agencies, shelters, and police can also assist in making necessary arrangements for teens to get a free bus ride home. The Home Free program has been operating since 1984 and has helped thousands of teens return to their families.[5]

to gain admittance. Placement in these shelters offers a cooling-down period for teens, and time for the county to decide what to do with them next. It can also be an acceptable place for teens who are awaiting court dates, sentencing, or transfer to foster care or group homes. The length of stay is generally short, often two months or less.

Some of the most successful programs for runaways offer a combination of all types of services: shelter, counseling, and 24-hour hotlines. This is the case in most of Wisconsin's counties. Serviced by twenty-four private, non-profit agencies belonging to the Wisconsin Association of Runaway Services, these counties have a high rate of success in dealing with the runaway problem. Ren Svanoe, program coordinator for the association, reports that only 15 percent of runaways involved with the program are repeat runaways. Svanoe says the agencies focus on "training kids to speak up to their parents without shouting and training parents to listen better. It seems to work well."[6]

Family Counseling

Counseling is a crucial step for runaways. Generally, treatment emphasizes family-oriented therapy if possible. Services are offered within a limited time frame, usually fifteen to thirty days. At the beginning, the runaway and the family are typically at a crisis point. The initial focus of treatment is to identify existing problems and establish communication among family members. It is essential that the home environment be stabilized. Drug and alcohol counseling can be explored if necessary and referrals given to other mental health, educational, and vocational services if needed.

*C*ounseling can be a crucial step for families that are going through a difficult time.

Kelly Pack, a licensed independent social worker at the Rehab Center in Mansfield, Ohio, explains her role in the beginning of the counseling process. "My job is [to be] a salesman. I have to give them the sales pitch on why it would benefit them to change."

Pack tries to make her clients as comfortable as possible. She states that developing rapport with them happens throughout the process. "I meet the client where the client is at. I look for things the client is sharing that I can tap into. Sometimes things just click. But if a teenager is slouched on the couch and doesn't want to talk, I might put away the pad and pencil and just play cards."

Because she knows the duration of counseling is limited, Pack strives to build stability for the

*S*pending time with a support person such as a grandparent, aunt or uncle, or teacher can be very helpful for teens.

client. "I want to find and include 'cheerleaders,' nonprofessional support people such as a favorite aunt, teacher, or school guidance counselor, to be there to help the kid succeed when I'm no longer involved," Pack says. "But I always leave the door open for [clients] to reconnect with me anytime they wish."

She admits her job is sometimes trying. "Seeing [what] these kids live with can be hard. Some have been through more in their short years of life than I've ever seen in my own." Part of her training is learning how to handle herself and deal with the emotional backlash from her job. She believes that "the success of a good counselor is the ability to tap into peer support. Sometimes I need to dump on another counselor saying, 'You can't believe what I just heard.' Sometimes . . . I just cry."[7] But however emotional counseling can be, it is essential—and often the only remaining hope of healing in some situations.

Family counseling is helping the Van Hecke family of Watertown, Wisconsin, deal with daughter Laurraine's runaway episode. The eighth grader, under pressure from arguments at home and conflicts at school, ran away with two other teens late one October night. Her parents, Dina and Tom, immediately began a frantic search for the trio. They put up posters, contacted the police and missing children's groups, and hired a private investigator.

With Laurraine missing, Dina relived the nightmare of her own runaway experience. At age seventeen, Dina left her New Mexico home and headed for Colorado and Wyoming. While on the run, she was beaten and raped. Dina was terrified for her daughter. "I thought, 'Oh my gosh, the same thing might happen to her. She might not get out alive.'"[8]

Fortunately Laurraine and her friends only went as far as Madison, a city about forty-five miles away. They stayed in various apartments and got food, marijuana, and alcohol from other runaways. On the fourth day of their run, they were picked up by the private investigator and one of Laurraine's four brothers. Laurraine admitted she was glad to go home. She says she did not drink or smoke pot while she was gone because she knew she was already in enough trouble.

Now Laurraine has succeeded in distancing herself from her troublesome friends. Her parents are pleased and relieved their daughter escaped any serious harm. "We're in family counseling so that we can all work on this together—so that our house is not one that you have to run away from," reports Laurraine's father. "We're family and we have to stick together. There's nothing that is more important to me than that."[9]

In order for counseling to be successful, the behavior or attitude of one or more of the parties involved must change. It is usually best for the adult to initiate the process and any reconciliation that needs to occur. Adult family members have the legal power and, hopefully, the emotional maturity to bring about the needed change. When adults do not do their part, success is unlikely. When they do, the results occur sooner and with more lasting effect.

Megan, at the age of fifteen, has already experienced years of problems with her mother. She was first taken from her home by social services at the age of thirteen, when she was declared a victim of child abuse. She was placed in foster care but ran away. Later, Megan was allowed to return to her mother. But she found herself in a dangerous situation. Her mother's steady boyfriend at the time would beat Megan. Now in a residential youth facility, Megan still maintains hope of reuniting with her mother, who is finally showing some effort at improving the situation and correcting her negligent behavior.

Megan says, "She finally met this other guy, and she's gotten a lot better. . . . She got her GED and she's going to college and she's going to graduate this year and she's a lot better mom than she was when I was little. She doesn't go out at all; she doesn't drink at all; I don't know if she still does pot at all."[10] Megan feels that with her mother's help there is a

*T*eachers who are supportive and willing to help students make up for lost time can make all the difference for a runaway returning to school.

chance of overcoming their problems and once again having a life together.

Returning to Home and School

Even after receiving professional help, returning to a normal life can be difficult for a runaway. The situation at home is likely to be strained. Parents may place the blame for this stress on the runaway. Parents may be experiencing emotions such as fear, anger, denial, or disbelief. Lines of communication opened through counseling may become damaged again. After the initial reunion, which may or may not have been happy, arguments can again arise.

The runaway also faces the challenge of returning to school. Dealing with questioning peers and missed schoolwork can be overwhelming. Runaways may also feel isolated from classmates and ashamed of their runaway experience. They sometimes make a show of bravado to avoid painful explanations.

Teacher's reactions are critical to the successful return of the student to school. A show of support and a willingness to help the student make up for lost time are two ways teachers can ease the runaway back into school life.

School counselors can be instrumental in helping with these predictably awkward transitions. By building trust with the runaway, the counselor can act as a guide and serve as a sounding board during the difficult reentry period. It is helpful for the counselor to coordinate school assignments and activities. The student should not be thrust into a hectic or hostile environment likely to lead to academic or social failure. The counselor can serve as a go-between, easing the pressure between the student and the teachers and peer groups.

Helping the runaway deal with other students is also crucial. Sometimes supervised group work is encouraged. It can be helpful for the runaway to talk to peers who have gone through similar experiences. Or they can help other students who are contemplating running away by giving them an accurate picture of what may happen to them. Runaways who are having trouble making friends may begin to feel connected to others by forming relationships within the group.

A runaway returning to home and school faces many obstacles. The goals for the teen should include improved understanding of his or her problems, better problem-solving skills, good academic performance, and a strengthening of relationships within the family. With help, these goals can be achieved.

Chapter 6

Before a Teen Runs

The decision to run is usually not an impulsive one. Most runaways struggle with the decision before acting on it. They view running away as a last resort. Running away does not necessarily mean that the teen has planned a permanent break with his or her family. In fact, runaways usually hope to reunite later with their loved ones.

Prevention is preferable to dealing with an intervention situation or the possibility of losing track of a runaway altogether. When symptoms exist it is crucial that they be taken seriously. School counselors, friends, and family members are often the first to recognize a potential problem. They can serve as a lifeline to the would-be runaway.

Signs of Risk

Difficulties experienced by the potential runaway usually cause a change in the teen's behavior. Poor academic performance at school, or a well-behaved student suddenly becoming rebellious or unusually

Warning Signs

There are many warning signs of a teen at risk—and a potential runaway. Although one or even several of the following signs could have various causes, they should not be ignored.[1]

Personality Changes: mood swings, irritability, changes in behavior

Signs of Depression: showing or expressing feelings of hopelessness and unworthiness

Sleep Changes: fatigue, insomnia, increased amount of sleep

Changes in Relationships: ignoring old friends, having a new set of undesirable friends

Withdrawal from Family Members: avoidance of family, growing isolation

School Problems: poor grades, disciplinary problems, truancy

Overreaction to Problems: prolonged reaction to loss or stress such as death, divorce, illness, or moving to a new city

Verbal Threats of Running: any statements about running away could be a cry for help and should be taken seriously

withdrawn, can indicate a problem. A drastic change in appearance or new relationships with undesirable peers can be another sign. Teens may exhibit impulsive behavior or extreme lack of patience. They may become angry and hostile toward their family. Their actions may be an attempt to get attention. Sometimes the teen will become involved in serious trouble such as taking drugs or breaking the law. The parents must not make the mistake of ignoring or denying these problems. To do so would be to deny the seriousness of the situation.

One San Diego, California, teen flunked her classes, popped pills, got caught shoplifting, and committed vandalism before running away. Her mother recalls how she and her husband reacted to this troubling behavior:

> We kept saying it was an early adolescent phase. She kept breaking rules and doing way-out things, and we kept telling ourselves that soon it would pass. We kept wanting to believe things weren't as serious as they really were.[2]

Intervention

Talk of running away is a cry for help. Regardless of reasons given by the teen for contemplating this action, physical or sexual abuse must be considered as a possible cause. It is of the utmost importance to determine whether or not protective custody is necessary. Sometimes a state child welfare agency needs to become involved immediately to ensure the teen's safety. It has the authority to take the steps necessary to remove a child from a dangerous situation.

Likewise, if the teen is contemplating a violent

act or threatening harm to himself or others, the authorities and the parents need to be informed immediately. The teen may feel betrayed or angry if such a step is taken, but it is necessary to avoid possible tragedy.

It is also advisable to draw the parents into counseling with the teen before the teen turns to running away as a solution. It is helpful for parents to be involved from the start, when problems are being identified. Even if the teen protests, the parents will have to be involved to bring about successful solutions. The parents need to realize and accept their role in what is, more often than not, a family problem.

Parental acceptance of this likelihood is not always forthcoming. Kelly Pack explains the importance of the family working as a unit:

> With me, I treat the family, I don't just treat the kid. I have better results when I'm attempting to fix the whole picture, not just one piece of the puzzle. Parents sometimes just want to plop the kid down and say, 'Here's the problem.' But usually something much bigger is going on.
>
> In my experience, kids usually want help. Some parents, when included in the picture of the problem, say ". . . No, it's the kid that's the problem, not us. . . ." I would challenge these parents to look at the picture as a whole and consider their role in the problem. I would say get into your kids' shoes. See things as they see them.[3]

School counselors, teachers, and others working with teens in any capacity need to have phone numbers, such as the National Runaway Switchboard, and other helpful information available to distribute if needed. Teens who feel a friend is in trouble and at risk of running should contact an adult for help.

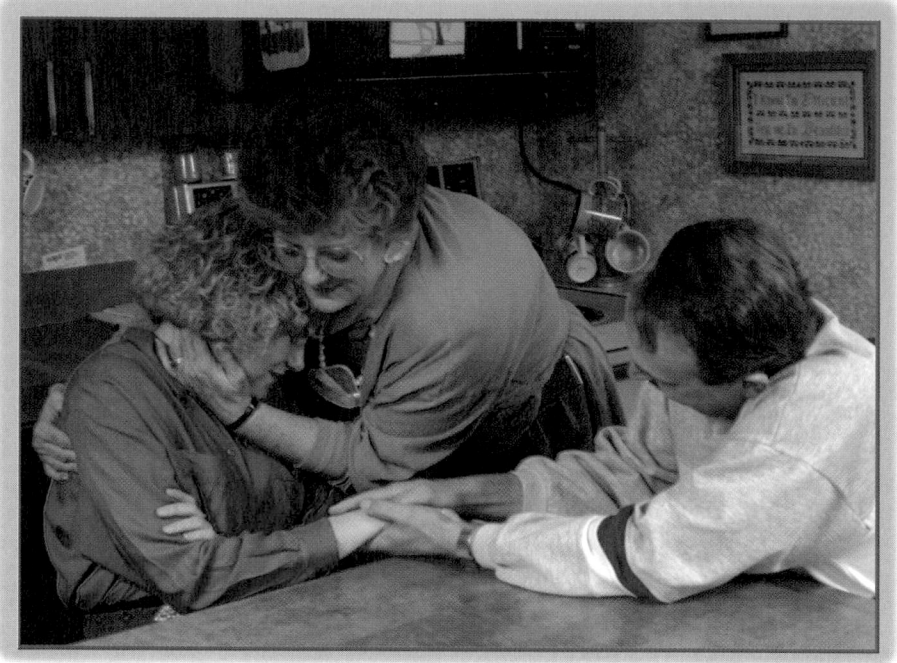

*P*arents and other family members can be very supportive, especially when they are approached for help with a genuinely serious problem.

Seeking Other Solutions

Before acting on the impulse to run away, there are steps for teens to consider that may help put their problems in perspective and lead to positive solutions. First of all, teens should assess their situation carefully to see if it really warrants running away. This includes examining every aspect of their life— home, family, friends, and school—and being honest about where the problems are and how severe they have become. Certain problems may seem more serious than they truly are.

Some teens overlook their parents or other family members as a source of help. Teens may not even try to talk about their feelings with their parents because they assume that their parents will not understand. But even parents who seem disinterested may prove to be very supportive when approached with a real problem. Another option may be for the teen to stay temporarily with a friend or relative until they sort out their problems and feelings. Teens can also suggest family counseling if they feel it is necessary.

If drugs or alcohol are a problem, help is available. Running away will not cure it. Support and rehabilitation can. Teens can make the smart choice.

Teens in abusive situations should seek help immediately from an adult or the authorities. Abuse is a crime. Teens do not have to continue to be victimized. Teens who do not know where to turn for help can contact a hotline to find out what is available in their area.

Teens who are thinking about running away should think about how difficult it would be to make it on their own. How would they eat? Where would they sleep? How would they earn money? Simple things, such as going to the bathroom or taking a shower, become complicated for teens out on the street. Finding ways to protect themselves from prostitution, drug abuse, disease, theft, and violence may become daily life-or-death issues.

Many resources exist to help troubled teens. Confidential hotlines or counseling are excellent options. It is important for teens to maintain control over their lives and the choices they make, and help is available. No teen needs to be on the street. If you or someone you know is thinking of running, be sure to run toward help instead of running away.

Hotlines

Greyhound Home Free Program
This program, which offers a free bus ride home for runaways, can be contacted through local police departments or through the National Runaway Switchboard at (800) 621-4000.

Lost Child Emergency Broadcast System
(317) 403-5059

National Center for Missing and Exploited Children
(800) THE-LOST or
(800) 843-5678

National Runaway Switchboard
(800) 621-4000

National Youth Crisis Hotline
(800) 448-4663

Safe Kids International
(888) 820-KIDS or
(888) 820-5437

Vanished Children's Alliance
(800) VANISHED or
(800) 826-4743

Chapter 1. A National Epidemic

1. Dee J. Hall, "Running from Home," *Wisconsin State Journal*, November 28, 1997, p. 1A.

2. "Running Away," *SIRS Digest*, Spring 1997.

3. Michael Rohr and Richard James, "Runaways," *School Counselor*, vol. 42, issue 1, September 1994, p. 40.

4. "Running Away."

5. Personal interview with Gordon J. Wendling, December 1, 1999.

6. Hall.

7. David Holmstrom, "On the Trail of a Wayward Daughter," *Christian Science Monitor*, vol. 91, issue 159, July 14, 1999, p. 13.

8. Ibid.

Chapter 2. Why Kids Run

1. "Running Away," *SIRS Digest*, Spring 1997.

2. David Holmstrom, "Teens Who Run from Troubled Families Find Help," *Christian Science Monitor*, vol. 87, issue 205, September 18, 1995, p. 12.

3. Frances K. Goldscheider and Calvin Goldscheider, "The Effects of Childhood Family Structure on Leaving and Returning Home," *Journal of Marriage and Family*, vol. 60, issue 3, August 1998, p. 745.

4. Personal interview with Gordon J. Wendling, December 1, 1999.

5. Laurie Schaffner, "Searching for Connection: A New Look at Teenaged Runaways," *Adolescence*, vol. 33, issue 131, Fall 1998, p. 619.

6. "Project Safe Place," n.d., <http://www.diogenesnet.com/Services/Safe_Place/safe_place.html> (October 21, 1999).

7. Schaffner.

8. Ibid.

9. Ibid.

Chapter 3. Throwaways

1. "Running Away," *SIRS Digest*, Spring 1997.

2. David Holmstrom, "Teens Who Run from Troubled Families Find Help," *Christian Science Monitor*, vol. 87, issue 205, September 18, 1995, p. 12.

3. "Running Away."

4. Dee J. Hall, "Running from Home," *Wisconsin State Journal*, November 28, 1997, p. 1A.

5. Laurie Schaffner, "Searching for Connection: A New Look at Teenaged Runaways," *Adolescence*, vol. 33, issue 131, Fall 1998, p. 619.

6. Antonia J. Martinez, "Think Before You Walk the Mean Streets," *Yes*, November 1994, p. 10.

Chapter 4. Life on the Streets

1. Donald Dale Jackson, "I Lost a Baby, and When I Got Him Back He Was a Toddler," *Smithsonian*, vol. 26, issue 7, October 1995, p. 70.

2. Jon D. Hull, "Running Scared," *Time*, vol. 144, issue 21, November 21, 1994, p. 92.

3. Jody M. Greene and Christopher L. Ringwalt, "Substance Use Among Runaway and Homeless Youth in Three National Samples," *American Journal of Public Health*, vol. 87, issue 2, February 1997, p. 229.

4. Hull.

5. Evan Karl Cutler, *Runaway Me: A Survivor's Story* (Fort Collins, Colo.: A Blooming Press, 1994), p. 313.

6. Hull.

7. Ibid.

8. Ibid.

9. Ibid.

10. Ibid.

11. "Streetcats Foundation," n.d., <http://www.slip.net/~scmetro/street.htm> (September 21, 1999).

12. Hull.

13. Ibid.

Chapter 5. Getting Help

1. Personal interview with Gordon J. Wendling, December 1, 1999.

2. "National Demographics," *Statistics*, 1998, <http://www.nrscrisisline.org/stats.htm> (September 14, 1999).

3. David Holmstrom, "Teens Who Run from Troubled Families Find Help," *Christian Science Monitor*, vol. 87, issue 205, September 18, 1995, p. 12.

4. "Running Away," *SIRS Digest*, Spring 1997.

5. "Home Free Program," 1997, <http://www.greyhound.com/Services/hmfrprog.html> (September 21, 1999).

6. Dee J. Hall, "Mom: My Daughter's Missing; Doesn't Anyone Care?," *Wisconsin State Journal*, October 28, 1997, p. 1A.

7. Personal interview with Kelly Pack, December 2, 1999.

8. Dee J. Hall, "Lesson Learned, Runaway Returns—Family Begins to Seek Help," *Wisconsin State Journal*, November 28, 1997, p. 4A.

9. Ibid.

10. Laurie Schaffner, "Searching for Connection: A New Look at Teenaged Runaways," *Adolescence*, vol. 33, issue 131, Fall 1998, p. 619.

Chapter 6. Before a Teen Runs

1. Based on "Tips for Parents," n.d., <http://www.diogenesnet.com/Services/Safe_Place/Tips_for_Parents/tips_for_parents.html> (October 21, 1999).

2. Myron Brenton, *The Runaways: Children, Husbands, Wives, and Parents* (New York: Penguin Books, 1978), p. 165.

3. Personal interview with Kelly Pack, December 2, 1999.

Ayer, Eleanor H. *Homeless Children*. San Diego, Calif.: Lucent Books, 1996.

Freman, David. *Running Away*. New York: Marshall Cavendish Corporation, 1995.

Greenberg, Keith E. *Runaways*. Minneapolis, Minn.: Lerner Publications, 1995.

Hyde, Margaret O. *Missing and Murdered Children*. New York: Franklin Watts, 1998.

Plona, Rebecca. *Drugs and Teen Runaways*. New York: Rosen Publishing Group, Inc., 1998.

Switzer, Ellen. *Anyplace but Here: Young, Alone and Homeless: What to Do*. New York: Simon & Schuster, 1992.

Tattersall, Clare. *Coping with Drugs, Runaways, and Teen Prostitution*. New York: Rosen Publishing Group, Inc., 1999.

Diogenes Runaway Information
<http://www.diogenesnet.com>

Greyhound Home Free Program
<http://www.greyhound.com/services/community.html>

Lost Child Emergency Broadcast System
<http://www.lostchild.net>

National Center for Missing and Exploited Children
<http://www.missingkids.org>

National Runaway Switchboard
<http://www.nrscrisisline.org>

Safe Kids International
<http://www.safekidsintl.com>

Streetcats Foundation
<http://www.slip.net/~scmetro/street.htm>

Vanished Children's Alliance
<http://www.vca.org>

Internet Addresses

Index